1

"True power is self-control." Joseph Bonanno

F.D.A. Approved Poetry by Michael Marrotti

The Inevitability Of Narcotics

I feel lethargy
catching up
after the long haul
on the prowl again
to replenish all
the pills I've eaten

Looking down
from the overlook
on Mt. Washington
until the stash
is depleted

Mummified in
wet blankets from
drops of sweat
forming a river
the size of Allegheny
all that awaits
is a couch
that feels like
concrete

I find myself
here periodically
desperate as
a convicted felon
pleading not guilty

Waiting for the bond
to reach ten percent
when every minute spent
feels like it'll be my last
one cage to another
living a life of fees
crawling out
of an orange bottle

Three Refills Remaining

I'm never late
for this date
the anticipation
of pleasure

We'll rekindle
this rebellion
against the
opposition

We're staggering
two steps ahead
authentic smiles
upon our faces

Guilty as charged
for the possession
of sustenance
we keep marching
in the right direction

One white cloud
away from
rectifying this
imbalance

Living like I mean it
loose pills rattling
inside my pockets
some say I have a
problem

I tell those
infidels
I have the
antidote

White Clouds Of Elation

Sneezing
out oxy
first thing
in the
morning

Walking
through a
white cloud
of elation

Climbing
the stairs
avoiding
the steps

Only a
follower
would
submit
to a
program

I'm making
progress
one day at
a time

All my faith
is consolidated
into a single
phone call

I often wonder
how the other
side lives

Able to accept
all the things
that drive

people to
madness

This renegade
is still free
to walk these
streets of
disease
without the
threat of
infection

This straw
is my sword

This bottle
my shield

Together we'll
fight of the
contamination
of societal
madness

Pharmaceutical Pleasure

I can smell it
from a block away
as the rain drips
from the dark skies
I can taste it

There's a
procedure
to be had
once I make
that journey
grinding it down
dust to dust

It goes hand
to hand with
a cigarette
all these
chemicals
to alleviate
the boredom

I'll finish this line
after I finish
the other

This is between
my dealer
my lovers
paycheck
and the will
to persist
when all other
options are futile

Misery Of Living

On a first
name basis
at my
hometown
pharmacy

Solace
is an
orange
bottle
that says
I still have
five refills
remaining

The same
faceless
people
accompany
me on the
trolley

I've witnessed
the benefits
of Christianity
at the
Light Of Life
but God is
still a stranger

All alone
amongst
the crowd
people carry on
like it makes
a difference

I failed
at the
wrong place

at the
right time

Travelled
every zip code
to find what
I was after

She was right
next door
to stitch
my wounds
of misery
I needed shelter
from the cold
streets of Dormont

I feel at one
when I'm in
her presence

In a way
I've conquered
the misery
of living

The Cleansing

Insomnia
will pass on
like a spirit
to the
underworld

Playing with
myself to
nullify the
absence
of touch

Using my arm
as an ashtray
wrapped up
in white sheets
that once held
your scent
now reek of
burning flesh

Playing fast
on this old
blue guitar
I'm three
song's away
from finishing
this set

Living my way
is a deserted
path of
identical
footsteps

After the
detoxification
of filthy
parasitic drugs

This little
departure
should be
easier than
a cam-girl
and clean
as a virgin

Whiteness Without The Guilt

Symmetrical
perfection
easily
concealed

Tranquility
in my
pocket
whiteness
without
the guilt

A bitter
taste that
contradicts
the bitterness
of the past

It lasts long
enough to
make it stop

For once
the clock
is my friend

The Cure

Piles of white pills
smothered
in vagina
I use the juice
of your love
to wash down
the excess

Pardon me
as I self indulge
two hands
and two options
multiple personalities
are easily entertained

Killing myself
to exist in a
capitalistic
society

Hedonism
is the
answer
fighting off
the angst of living
preoccupied by
my own pleasures

Fight Of My Life

I've
swallowed
thousands
of pills

Fucked the
finest pussy
in Pittsburgh

Talked for hours
to the most
prestigious
shrinks available

Expressed
my contempt
through countless
fist fights
sometimes I won
even though
it feels like
I'll never truly win

I've drank
myself sober
I've fallen
up stairs

DMT worked
like a charm
I smoked
that shit until
I woke up alone
perspiration
my only friend

I've tried over
and over again
no matter what
avenue I travel

regardless of
what company
I keep

Life has
a tendency
to come out
on top

It's a losing battle
I never seem to win

Insufficient Funds

I see you
through
drowsy
eyes

Embrace
you from
the depths
of my
blissful
soul

Feel you
as the one
worthy of
this urine
erection

We share
thoughts
that are
triggered
through the
benevolence
of chemistry

We'll run
this course
down to the
last line

Then sleep
in harmony
fulfillment
is ours

It's a
redundant
cycle
that keeps

spinning
on high

Until that
fateful day
when the
balance
displays
those words

Insufficient
funds

No Connection

They might
as well
start digging
the ditch

The inevitable
has arrived
leaving me
incapacitated

This time
of peace
those
perpetual
white clouds
have fled
from above
I'm in the
wrong zip code

The storm
is here
I've had to
pardon myself
of this
chemical smile
a shutoff notice

Out to make
a connection
when the Wi-Fi
is turned off
it start from
the legs
working it's
way up

If all it took
was a switch

I'd turn it on high

I've always
embraced
the future
now I'm
left with
nothing but
nostalgia

Orange Is The New White

Orange
is the
new white
I'm much
obliged
to have
made your
acquaintance

I apply
pressure
turning
like a
democrat

White residue
on my hands
the stabilization
of shaky fingers

Three strikes
down the
hatch

Capitulation

It says
to take one
every four
to six hours

I'm lonely as is
and terrible at
following directions

My Brain Without Drugs

Secluded
on a dead end road
exceeding the speed limit
with no detour in sight
left with no options
forced to accept my fate
I spit in my hand
as I caress
my disappointed penis
in the hopes of saying
hello to solace

Much to my despair
I couldn't even acquire
a state of pre-cum

Approaching the end
with a limp dick
I gotta say for the most part
I enjoyed the ride
nothing says achievement
like time well wasted

Wasted I was

Living off fried rice
candy bars and
the occasional orgasm
was good enough for me
when I had my milligrams

The sign I just passed
said there's only seven
miles left to go

Nostalgia kicks in as I
recall my favorite destination

Destination flaccid avenue

Money exchanges
pockets full of goodies
rejoice!
another day I avoided
demon dope sick

Scratching myself to sleep
scratching myself awake
lucid dreams
panic in Dormont

It was only a matter of time
unfortunately
that time came too soon

Only four miles left
and my nose begins to run
the price a man gotta pay
for happiness is tragic

Only two miles left
my body is introduced
to agony
she's a merciless cunt
why did I do this
to myself

Only one mile left
I've lost the will to persist

This is my brain without drugs

Life Is So Alluring

My prescription
is filled on
the first
of each month
like clockwork

Rent is
always paid
in full by
the fifth

By the end
of the month
I'm having
manic episodes
that are oftentimes
detrimental to
those who
accompany me

All my neighbor
talks about
is work
it never fails

The folks
who moved in
across the street
drink Mexican beer
each and every
Sunday night
they always have
monotonous
reggae music blaring
in the background

Each time
they spot me
out on the porch

enjoying
a cigarette
on the day
of rest
with my
latest novel
they invite me
over for a drink

I always
politely decline
drinking has lost
it's charm
but I'll tell you what
a decade ago
I would've drank
away this imbalance

Transcendence

There was a time
when the sun shined
the bird's flew
amongst the bee's

Star's were close
enough to reach
and the one
piece of ass
I had was good
enough

It was the day
before my
prescription
ceased to be
the day I was
high enough
to touch God

Prayers would
have never
ascended me
as high as this

The pious
are foolish
for believing
otherwise

A Critical Self-Analysis

If I were a little
more dishonest
smiling when I
didn't mean it
offering praise
instead of candor
I'd have more friends

If my penis had
a few more inches
got off sooner
than later and
lowered it standards
I'd have more lovers

If my dealer would
lower his prices
picked up the phone
when I wanted
and didn't behave
like a green eyed
bastard
I'd be less unstable

If these words
weren't so fluent
profound and
proactive
worthwhile and
clever
by the standards
of the small press
my book of poems
would've been
published

Take One Three Times A Day

Chemicals flow
down the stream
of disorder

Dissolving in a
matter of minutes
a mitigation of
countless hours

Contradicting
these caustic feelings
they've been by
my side throughout
this tumultuous journey

I'm a fucking mess
but I'm inhibited
in this moment

I agree there's
a problem
that supersedes
another

This dependency
is slavery
but it's the only
form I know
that offers
emancipation

The Chemical Rebellion

Today was an
extraordinary day
it wasn't like the rest
those others days
just sucked

Sucked the life
right out of you

But not today
for the
prescription
is near

With this bottle
and these straws
we rebel against
the atrocities of
this callous planet

In solidarity we blow
like the wind
to separate ourselves
from the filth

We blow like a hurricane
until we transcend
looking down
upon them

We blow until our minds
are expunged of all
deplorable human
characteristics

Blowing it away
euphoria, sweet euphoria
it's extraordinary
days like these
that even the losers
have an opportunity
to win

Two Disorders Don't Make A Right

I've been standing naked
in front of a mirror
for years
fucking myself
a synonym
is not the answer

I'd rather
export my penis
place it gently
after all
it's highly important
on a disinfected
solitary shelf

Than deal
with anyone
who shares
these similarities
the thought alone
has me popping pills

Two lunatics
on the same
mood stabilizers
no balance to be had
on these unstable grounds

I'm already nuts
you're cuckoo
for pills
the size of coco puffs
this is nothing more
than a bipolar affair

I heard
yeah sometimes
I hear voices
they said
you have new jacket
it's a real tight fit

Tranquility isn't
an easy thing to attain
I know its uncomfortable
here's me
with a chemical smile
congratulations

After all this time
in psychiatric care
a manifestation
in a white room
they told me its yours
and I told them
time is of the essence
that fucking crazy bitch
can keep it all to herself

Jesus Is Not Needed

Jesus isn't needed
in my heart
to become
a better person
opening that door
would only close
another
like the door
to my dealer

This wallet
is opened
blood is flowing
the heart
is beating
like a drum
no need
to pray
when those prayers
go unanswered
my dealer
never ignores me
always picks
up the phone

No delusions
only truth
my faith
in this feeling
though costly
is liberating
to have faith
in you
is to renounce
control

This
megalomaniac
is repulsed
by the thought
of ever walking
down that

straight and narrow
suppressive road

Better Living Through Chemistry

Is it gonna rain
or shine
I can't get the answers
in this dubious lifestyle
people keep speaking
words they don't mean
here I am
stuck in between
now I'm indecisive

The time
keeps ticking by
aging like cheap wine
I've come
to a conclusion
an important decision
think what you want
I've made up my mind

Ring ring from my iPhone
boredom is
tantamount to confusion
my dealer said
he'd swing on by
hours later
the police intervened
another surprise
fuck my life
showing up uninvited

It's a city of confusion
I say this ambiguously
the only thing
that's for sure
is the chemicals
and refills
inside of this little bottle
better living
in Pittsburgh
through the benevolence
of chemistry

I Thought Everything Was Fine

I'm anxious
I'm depressed
help me

I've swallowed
my required dose
took bonus drugs as well
still I'm burdened
with a feeling
who has no right
to intrude
on my otherwise
sublime state
of mental health

Things are wonderful
for me I suppose
I can find a problem
in that
when there's no issues
to be had
maybe I've had enough

Obsessing
in a negative way
knowing
what brings me pleasure

Pessimistic
optimistic
right now
I'm being unrealistic
and I hate my thoughts for it

My mind
is playing tricks on me
as I surf the waves
of this imbalance
trying my hardest
not bail out

Ride it out

let it be
what I need
is a in between peace
and a calming silence

Between The Lines

I've seen the signs
read between the lines
made my purchase
the lines ceased to be

Happiness manifested
I watched the signs
glow and blur as I
climbed the ladder
to where I once was

Transcendence

I'm on top
of the situation
looking down
on the upside
hijacking these
lazy endorphins
forcing them to
work a double
setting myself up for
a significant moment
signing away my release

The Drought

I've been stuck
in a tunnel for seven days
looking for a glimpse
of sunshine
or a feeling that once was
if only I could replace
lethargy with lucky
I'd be one step closer
to my favorite destination

The more I travel
the more I lose touch
with who I was
where I was going
and what I've become

Reluctantly working
for my own independence
this is a fateful choice
I would never voluntarily
choose

Here I stagger
as I attempt
to get straight
in every crooked path
or faithless thought
denouncing
my self inflicted struggle
crawling like the parasites
who capitalize off others
until they reached their peek

I'll get back to the top
if I have to construct
my own ladder

Michael Marrotti is an author from Pittsburgh using words instead of violence to mitigate the suffering of life in a callous world of redundancy. His primary goal is to help other people. He considers poetry to be a form of philanthropy. When he's not writing, he's volunteering at the Light Of Life homeless shelter on a weekly basis.

Made in the USA
San Bernardino, CA
13 October 2016